The One Hundred Year Old Man I Met In China:
A Long Poem About An Old Taoist Who Lives
On A Mountaintop In Dongbei Close To North Korea
and Russia or the Old CCCP And Who Told Me
The Secrets Of Happiness, Health, And Longevity

Martin Avery

Dedication: To The 100 Year Old Man I Met In China
ISBN #978-1-312-38850-5
Copyright © Martin Avery, 2014

If you can conceive of an unnameable infinite power (call it Tao) that has always existed, that powers the universe, holds molecules together, makes the flowers bloom, birds sing, your heart beat, allows some things to evolve while others don't, allows the sun to shine and rain to fall on both the good and the evil, all without putting any demands on the recipients or having the need to be worshiped or even acknowledged... then you might be a Taoist. -- youmightbeataoist.com

If you have a hard time reconciling proven historic and scientific facts with contradictory stories passed down by uneducated superstitious desert dwellers, edited and re-edited by generations of religious and government leaders for their own benefit, constantly quoted out of context by followers with their own agendas, about a god who's described as jealous, petty, indecisive, and ruthless, having murdered millions, including admittedly innocent victims... you might be a Taoist. -- youmightbeatoaist.com

The One Hundred Year Old Man I Met In China:
A Long Poem About An Old Taoist Who Lives
On A Mountaintop In Dongbei Close To North Korea
and Russia or the Old CCCP And Who Told Me
The Secrets Of Happiness, Health, And Longevity

Martin Avery

The One Hundred Year Old Man I Met In China

When I moved to China, in the autumn of 2014, I met a man who
looked like me, I thought, a guy who could be my double, an old
Taoist priest, my size, my age, I thought, who looked like me, if
I was Chinese, but I found out he was actually much older.
He was twice my age: he was exactly one hundred years young.
He was born in 1915, a few years before my father, who was
long gone, but the Chinese guy told me that he wasn't really
sure of his year of birth because in China they go by the lunar
calendar, which makes things a little different, but the exact year
wasn't the interesting or important thing, he told me, it was the
fact that he had a strange affliction that made him appear, and
feel, half his age. "It was awkward when I was ten and I looked
five, he said, "and when I was twenty and I looked ten, but then
again it was alright when I was forty and I looked twenty and
better when I was sixty and looked thirty and look at me now,
twice as old as you but most people would guess we're the same age.

Is there a name for this affliction? I asked. Is there a cause?
Can it be duplicated, or replicated? We could make a lot of
people happy, if it can, and if we can sell it, we'll make a lot of
money. And that made him laugh. He said a number of doctors
had checked him out, over the years, and they said he was just
lucky, it wasn't genetic or caused by the environment or anything
he ate, and it wasn't because his body was out of balance, as the
Traditional Chinese Medicine doctors say, in fact, he had good
"jing-chi-shen", which means he was healthy, had good energy,
and would live a long time. Also, he confided, I dye my hair,
as a lot of older men in China do. -- At least you're not like
Benjamin Buttons, aging in reverse, I said, although I didn't
think he would know the movie I was talking about. -- I saw that,
he said. The movie about the guy who looked old when he was
born and kept on getting younger, physically, but not mentally,
util he was dead. -- You watch Hollywood movies? I said.

One of the first things I did when I moved to China was find a doctor for Traditional Chinese Medicine and she was the one who introduced me to the 100 year old man. She gave me the full treatment, with acupuncture, fire cupping, tunai or finger needling, moxibustion, herbal teas and patches, even burning moxa on acupuncture needles for the warm needle effect, so I would have better jing-chi-shen, and she told me all about the theory that went along with the treatments, the philosophy and history behind it, how TCM developed along with the spiritual and intellectual movements close to the heart of China: Taoism, Buddhism, and Confucianism. She explained that TCM had been around for five or six thousand years and she had been trained in Western medicine as well as Eastern medicine, but specialized in Traditional Chinese Medicine, and loved it, and her clinic mixed the best of the East and West, her mother and aunt were doctors trained in the Western tradition and her husband was trained in the Eastern tradition, and she had worked in the U.S.A. for several years in addition to her years in China. She graduated at the very top of her class at Beijing University, which is at the very top of rankings of universities in China. So, when she asked me if I wanted to meet and interview a one hundred year old man who looked fifty, I did not hesitate to say "Yes" and I did not waste any time asking stupid questions like "Are you sure he's 100" or "How do you know he's 100?" or anything like that. Besides, she showed me a copy of his birth certificate, not that I asked for it, and I thought doctors weren't supposed to show you things like that, but in China there is a little less concern for privacy than we are used to in the conservative West, so I didn't make a big deal about it.

My doctor contacted the 100 year old man on Wee Chat, which is a Chinese version of MSN or Facebook chat, and he agreed to meet me at the ancient Taoist temple on top of the mountain in the middle of the city where we lived, in the Development Zone of Dalian, or the Kaifaqu section, on the mountain we call Big Monk or Grand Monk Mountain and they call Daheishan. If you look it up online you will see they say Daheishan is the Taoist holy land. It's not a famous place promoted all over the world or across China or even in Dalian but Taoism is like that: If you are in the flow and in the know, you'll find out all about it, and if you aren't interested in things like that, you'll never hear about it or notice it, even if it's right in front of your face, like Big Monk Mountain. Dalian had a population of around six million when I met the old guy, but it was growing fast, and every day the commuter train called the cin-guay, pronounced ching-way, took thousands of people right past the big black mountain, with lots of good views and long views and very few obstructions but I noticed that hardly anybody other than me even glanced in that direction. I took pictures of it and made little videos showing the approach to the mountain from both sides, from the train, and made more movies as I took a taxi or a motorcycle taxi up the mountain to the ancient temple to meet with the old guy and continue our interview.

There are several old temples on Daheishan, or Big Monk
Mountain, and a number of them are linked by a hiking trail
feature one thousand three hundred stone steps, and that
trail is known for its spiritual qualities, and they say it is
good for spiritual cleansing, as you hike through a beautiful
wilderness area from one temple to another to another and
if you go in to one or all of them you will discover some of
the history of Taosim and Buddhism in China and see how
they joined forces at one time and grew together for a while
so that now the temples are Buddhist Taoist temples or
Taoist Buddhist temples and some show a little influence of
Confucianism, too, but the temple where the old guy wanted to
meet me was on another part of the mountain, a short taxi
ride away, hidden in a little valley of a plateau near the top of
Daheishan, and they said it was so ancient that it actually
pre-dated Taoism as it was built in the era before Taoism
got started as a place where the local folk religion or
spiritual movement was celebrated and then it was taken over
and developed by Taoists and then knocked down several
times during different wars in different eras as the region was
occupied by the Mongol Empire, the CCCP or USSR, and
Imperial Japan, as well as Korea, earlier in history, and it
was known as Manchuria for a long time and now it is part
of China, again, as it was in the beginning, and for most of
the time of the Middle Kingdom known in the west as The
People's Republic of China. Dalian, they say, is a new city,
especially by Chinese standards, as the Russians designed it
around one hundred years ago, with a dream of making it
the Paris of the USSR, and the Japanese developed it, with
a fainter dream of making it the Paris of mainland Japan,
and now the Chinese are turning it into the capital of the
New China so it is known as the Hong Kong of the North or
the Paris of China. Daheishan, Grand Monk Mountain, and
the ancient temple on the mountain, watch the empires
come and go, come and go, like a patient anaesthtized on
an operating table, hoping to be left alone, or rebuilt
better, and right now it looks like a temple designed by
Escher as it has a lot of stairs going up and down and it's
easy to get lost going from one small temple to another
in the compound and it looks as though some of the
stairways are optical illusions or they incorporate optical

illusions so that if you saw someone walking sideways or upside-down you would not be too surprised, or any more surprised than you are to see a tree with golden leaves and a little furnace where they say they make pills that are good for longevity, as you see in so many Taoist temple compounds, or a big Buddha or Laughing Buddha sitting alongside the fierce-looking dieties of Taoism. Some people are surprised when they see dieties in a Taoist temple. What do dieties have to do with Taoism? they ask.

The answer is, Taoism, like Buddhism, is a little different in the East and in the West.

I looked at him, he looked at me, and it was plain
to see we both looked shocked, the way you do when
you see yourself in the mirror at midnight, when you
see your double, or recognize someone else the way
you recognize yourself, although you also recognize
they are completely different, as he was a 100 year old
Chinese guy and I was a Caucasian half his age; he was
a Taoist priest from China and I was a writer and
a teacher from Canada; he was about five foot
eleven, had a thin beard, and long black hair
pulled back on his head, and skin some would say
was yellow; I was the same
height, had a thick beard, trimmed short, thinning
hair, and skin most would say was white; we both had
big shoulders, big arms, big legs, size twelve shoes,
and dressed in black and white. Anyone who watched
us when we met must have seen quite a sight as two
guys from the opposite sides of the planet looked at
each other as though they had seen their long lost
twin brother from another mother and race.

The 100 year old man must have taken some of those
longevity pills, I decided, because he looked no older than
me and everybody said I was a young fifty. My doctor said
I was as strong and healthy as a man half my age, my
biological age was around twenty-four. The old monk
was 100 going on 50, everybody said. He looked lively
for an age most people look dead. He corrected me.
Most people my age are dead, he said. Any questions?

I had a lot of questions for the old guy but I didn't
ask them all at once. We met several times over a
few months, first in the ancient temple on Daheishan
and then I had to travel up north to where he lived,
on another mountain, in an area where you could see
North Korea and Russia, while still in China, and he
had a lot of things to say about that, as well as the
meaning of life, the secret of happiness, and a
little bit about my own life, and Canada, too. But
first I had to find a translator, as he spoke as much
English as I spoke Chinese, which was not much.

At that point, I spoke what they call 'taxi
Chinese', which means I knew enough Chinese
to get around town by taxi, with the help of
bilingual business cards.

The old man told me the most amazing story
about a life lived that included experience with three
empires: He had seen the British Empire come and
go, the American Empire wax and wane, the
Soviet Empire spread and contract, Imperial
Japan arrive and leave, and China rule the region,
go down hard, then get ready to lead the world.
But that wasn't the part that interested me the most.

I had lived in the U.K. and the U.S.A., then moved
to China, so I thought I knew where he was coming
from. But when he started talking about what he
had done and seen in his life, in this life, and then
in past lives and future lives, my mind was completely
blown. I've done a lot of past life work and had a
sense of some of my past and future lives, including
several in China, but this guy walked around with
a such a strong sense of who he was in the past,
present, and future it was like he had a working
knowledge of dozens of lives in different times and
he also had the ability to see who I was in the
past and present and future. Namaste, I said.
I see you and I have a great deal in common
even though we have never met and have nothing
much in common in this life. He laughed a little
and then told me some of the most amazing
things I have ever heard.

He made tea and we drank it slowly, sitting
meditatively in a special part of the ancient
Taoist compound, in a little pagoda, painted
beautifully, in primary colours, on a square
island of concrete surrounded by big koi
ponds filled with the decorative fish we call
brocaded carp, or big goldfish, in the West,
and behind him was a wall decorated with a
mural that turned into a three-dimensional
sculpture of a dragon that looked quite real.
The old Taoist temple compound was built around
a spring, high in the mountains, and if you crawled
through a tunnel to a cave there was a great place
for meditation where the spring water echoed
and reverberated but we preferred sitting outside
when the weather was good, as it always was,
surrounded by the beautiful fish in the ponds
with the dragon fresco as a backdrop.
Many years ago, the monks had channeled the
spring water so it poured out of the
dragon's mouth, into the koi pond, making
a beautiful noise. As the 100 year old
Taoist guy talked, my attention sometimes
wandered to the dragon spitting into the
koi pond and I got the impression it was the
dragon talking to me, instead of the old guy,
but I would give my fuzzy head a shake and
come back to the hear and now to discover
the guy twice was my age was twice as
focused as I was. The first thing I asked him
was the question cartoon characters always
ask the wise old guru on the mountain top:
What is the secret of life? What is the meaning
of life? But I framed it slightly differently.

You're so happy, I said. What is your secret.
People often ask me that, I added, and they
say I'm the happiest, most positive, person
they've ever met, and they want to know
why, and some people complain about it,
at work, saying it always looks like I'm having
more fun than they are, and they don't
like that, and my critics call me a blissed out
idiot or say I'm so happy I'm not in my
right mind. But I've worked at it, over the
years, to fight depression, keep the blues
far away, to find happiness, joy, bliss,
even ecstasy, every day. I went to a workshop
with the woman who wrote Everyday
Ecstasy and thought I could write a
better book called Ecstasy Every Day.

The 100 Year Old Man smiled slightly and
nodded his head and he said, Taoism is
all about health and happiness, as well as
longevity. If you are going to live a long time,
you want to be happy, of course, because
one hundred years of unhappiness would be
hard to bear and happiness inspires you
to live longer and do the things that make
you happier. And speaking of sex, he said,
alluding to Everyday Ecstasy, by Margot
Anand, the Taoist Bedroom Arts are
no secret but they are not as famous as
the Kama Sutra or the Ananga Ranga or
the Joy Of Sex or even that new movie
with Carman Diaz called Sex Tapes. The
Taoist Bedroom Arts, described in a
series of books by Mantak Chia, now living
in the U.S.A., describe different ways to
make love that are spiritual and healing,
designed to balance male and female
energy, and they include ways of
meditating together, especially in the
morning, as well as making love using
a formula known as the sixes and the

nines, not to be confused with sixty-nine
which is a Western version of the
black and white symbol of Taoisim
used to illustrate the principle that there are
two sides to everything in the universe,
dark and light, hot and cold, up and down,
and so on and on and on, and that's what
traditional Chinese medicine is based on,
rather than germs and disease and
drugs and surgery, it's all about
bringing the mind and body together
and back into balance. But you
probably know all that stuff, he said.

Making love, he went on, if you do it
in the way described in the Taoist
Bedroom Arts, also leads to happiness
and inspires you to live a long life and
do all the healthy things that help you
live a long life. The Taoist Bedroom Arts
were created and developed by women
a long time ago to tell men what they
want, which is still a big mystery to
men in the West, but these women
explained centuries ago. Their books
were written in a time when men
kept harems and had to keep a number of
women happy and more recently some of
that information has been given a new
life by Hollywood movies such as
Bliss, starring Terrence Stamp as a
relationship counsellor and sex
therapist, but that movie did not
do so well, probably because the
producers tacked on a long ending
that was all about sexual abuse,
which should have been a separate
movie, all on its own.

I nodded my head and said,
Where and when were you born,
old man who watches Hollywood movies
on a mountaintop in China?

The 100 Year Old Man said,
I was born here about a century ago.
The exact date, I don't know.

Where have you been? I asked him. Did you
travel? Have you been around the world? Asia? China?
Dongbei? North-eastern China? Lioaning,
the province we're in? Dalian? Do you ever
leave the temple compound and go down
the mountain called Daheishan, into
Kaifaqu or Dalian, take a plane from
Dalian Skyport to Seoul, Korea; Tokyo,
Japan; Beijing or Shanghai, Hong Kong
or Taipei; Australia or New Zealand;
North America, South America, Europe,
Africa?

100 Year Old Man: I've spent most of this life
right here on Daheishan, the place you call
Grand Monk Mountain or Big Black Mountain
in the middle of the part of Dalian they call
Kaifaqu, and another temple compound on
another mountain further to the north an east,
up by the borders with Korea and Russia.

Marty: So what do you remember or recall best
of all the time you were here during the era of
the British Empire, when this was Port Arthur,
when the British had a toe-hold in China they
wanted to use to gain entry into the spice and
other markets to trade and grow rich? What was
it like here, for you, in that time?

100 Year Old Man: Dalian was a place called
Port Arthur and there were many people here from
around the world so we saw faces and heard
languages from all over the place, including
the white faces of English-speaking men with
round, blue, eyes as well as Russians, Japanese,
Koreans, and people from other places in
Europe who spoke languages that sounded

nothing like English. I was five years old in
1920, fifteen years old in 1930, and the world
inside and outside of China changed enormously,
in those years, but I was just a boy, so I didn't
understand what it all meant, I just had a strong
feeling were in the middle of the world, if not
the universe, as everybody all over the world
wanted to travel here and trade with us, so we
had all sorts of products from around the world
and we gave away tonnes of spices and something
called opium that my father and his father said
they did not want me to know too much about.

Marty: What about the Boxer Rebellion and
the Opium Wars?

100 Year Old Man: We did not call it The Boxer
Rebellion, we called it by its proper name, or by
the name of the movement that led to the war
with Western countries, and that movement was
not about boxing, it wras about Chinese martial
arts. I trained with the closed hand society and
learned to fight, got into fighting shape, learned
how to dodge bullets, and moved from the
country into the city to spread the word about
our movement, which was all about keeping
China Chinese and keeping all the foreigners
out, or kicking them out, or just killing them
all, before we traded away everything that was
ours and made us what we were. But in the end
soldiers from all over the West worked together
to defeat us and not only did they beat us but
they beat China down so that it took decades
to recover.

Marty: And what do you remember about the
World Wars, the Korean War, and the Cold War?

100 Year Old Man: What you call the First
World War did not have as much impact here
as elsewhere in the world and it was nothing
compared to the Second World War, which
saw the end of the British Empire and the
start of the American Empire. I don't want to
talk about the Korean War or the long horrible
war against the Japanese Imperialists who
invaded China and took over this part of the
country. But I can say that it was hell, those
wars in this place were hell on Earth, and
they left China weaker and weaker, but
Dalian rebounded, especially when the Russians
were here, when Russia wasn't just Russia, when
it was the CCCP or the USSR, the Union of Soviet
Socialist Republics, a communist empire
stretching from the North Atlantic to the
North Pacific, a brutal regime with an
enormous system of prison camps across
Siberia, to the north of us, where thousands
and thousands of Russians were sent from
Moscow and other cities in Russia for
all kinds of crime, from the petty to the
political, and they built a railway from
St. Petersburg or Moscow all the way out here
and called this place Dalian, which means
far away, as it was as far away from Moscow
as you could get and still be in the USSR,
and their totalitarian regime was ruled by
fierce dictators, Stalin and Lenin, who quoted
Marx and did whatever they wanted, over-
throwing the old czars and a feudal society
to free the serfs or peasants and force them
into the future with an industrial revolution
and technological development that
amazed us, here in Dalian, what we heard
of it, and what we saw of it, as the Ruskies
tried to rebuild and re-invent Dalian as

the Paris of Russia or the Paris of the
Soviet Union or Paris, CCCP, or Paris,
USSR, which did not have a ring to it, but
they planned our streets and parks with
traffic circles and radial roads and big
open space, unlike anything in China, and
they built those roads and Russian buildings
and then walked away, after making a big
deal with the Japanese. And we never loved
the Russians when they occupied Manchuria
but we didn't want them to leave if the
Japanese were going to replace them, but
maybe that was good, in a way, because
the Chinese people were moved, inspired,
determined, to get the Japanese out of
China, in a way they were never motivated to
remove the Soviets, so that era of
occupation was difficult, then became
brutal, but the wars ended with Dalian
back in the hands of the Chinese people,
the way it was for centuries, before I was
born, before this lifetime, I mean ....

Marty: You remember your previous
lifetimes?

100 Year Old Man: I "remember"
past and future lives the way I remember
the thing that happened in this life, over
the past century, with considerable
clarity, sometimes, and with some things
I believe are better off forgotten. But there
was one life, one time, about two thousand
years ago, that you might like to hear about.

Marty: You remember a previous life from
around two thousand years ago? That was
the time of ....

100 Year Old Man: Jesus! You don't think
I'm going to tell you that Jesus spent his
so-called "lost years" in China and I met him
in a previous life and taught him everything
he needed to know in order to go back to
his part of the world and work as a healer
and public speaker inspiring his people to
rise up against the occupying army from
Rome as well as their own religion and
leaders and change their world completely
with a series of miracles and magical
events ranging from walking on water to
raising the dead and including making
lunch for the masses out of just a few
fish and loaves of bread?

Marty: You know that story, the whole
story, about Jesus, Jews, Christians, the
Bible, the Old Testament, the New
Testament, here, in China, where you've
lived your whole life, holed up in an
ancient Taoist temple compound on a
mountain called Daheishan or Big Monk
Mountain?

100 Year Old Man: Of course I know that
story. Everybody knows that story. People
have been telling that story for centuries,
making movies and TV shows, holding
weekly meetings, standing on street corners,
telling that story, proselatizing, telling
everyone who would listen that they have
to learn all about that religion in order to
reach salvation and go to heaven instead of
hell and they have to follow the ten
commandments and more precepts you get from
reading the psalms, parables, stories, in those
books and the commentaries on those books
and singing the songs and listening to
sermons and going to church and becoming
part of a little community and a big
community of people who believe in
all those stories about the guy who died
for his people and was born again a
few days later and then rose up into
heaven to be with his father who was
the god of the universe.

Marty: Well, when you put it that way,
it sounds sort of hard to believe, and
I thought that story was suppressed
over here for the past half century or so
or half your lifetime.

100 Year Old Man: China, like India,
the Indians of North America, the
people of South America, and Russia,
or the old CCCP or USSR, as well as
Japan, the Koreas, most of Africa,
and most of the world, live outside of
the Judeo-Christian culture you are
talking about, and we know there is no
such thing as Judeo-Christian culture,
Jews and Christians are quite different,
like Buddhists and Taoists, and the
Buddhists and Christians have a lot in

common, it appears, as though Jesus
and Buddha were brothers, and it
boggles the minds of some Christians
to think their religion isn't the only
one or the best or that the rest of
the world must have a problem if
they can't follow the story and become
followers of that religion that preaches
peace, humility, and cooperation but
has inspired so many wars over the
past two thousand years ....

Marty: Oh yeah, you're a Taoist, so
you don't believe in the big book full of
sexist, racist, misogynistic fairy tales
from the desert handed down from
illiterate fishermen through a long series
of kings, dictators, and other rulers who
had the stories edited for their own
purposes, to rule their people, and put down
women, foreigners, outsiders, the rest of
the world they wanted to conquer, and
is still used today as billions of people
go to church to sing and pray and
listen to sermons or, as the American
comedian George Carlin liked to say,
go to a building to check out
other people's clothing in the most
competitive way ....

The 100 Year Old Man said, Tell me about
your past lives, so I told him I had done a lot of
past life work and discovered I had many lives
in Europe, in the past, relating to the
Holocaust, and I had several lives in China,
including one or two in which I worked on
The Book Of The Dead and one in which I
was a lot like the Laughing Buddha, and one
in which I met Marco Polo and one in which
I worked with Dr. Henry Norman Bethune,
the doctor from Canada who brought

Western medicine as well as electricity to
a part of China that had seen neither during
the time of the Japanese invasion and the
start of the Communist revolution, and I had
several lives in which I was a Chinese woman,
including one in which I had bound feet and
future lives in which .... But he cut me off
because nobody talks about their future lives.

Me: What about your other past and future lives?
I asked the 100 Year Old Man.

He was starting to remind me of the
Two Thousand Year Old Man played by
the Jewish comedian Mel Brooks, from
time to time, in stand-up routines, years
ago, and recorded on old vinyl long playing
albums, or LPs, taking on the persona of
this old guy who talked about the old days
when kids played with sticks and the
only jobs were breaking rocks and it
sounded as though he must have been
a six thousand year old man .... Imagine
being six thousand years old and a
witness to everything in recorded history,
how that would change your perspective,
like studying history by living through
all of it ....

The 100 Year Old Man told me this story:
In a previous life, around two thousand
years ago, I was living in China and working
as a doctor, practicing traditional Chinese
medicine, of course, I mean, what else
was there, and I met a man who said he
came from the Middle East and was in
the Far East to learn all he could about
healing and related things and he wasn't
the white-skinned, fair-haired, blue-eyed,
tall, thin, English or Scandinavian looking
guy pictured in the books for children
describing the Bible and the life of Jesus,
he was dark-skinned as anyone from
Africa or the people living beside the
Mediterranean Sea between Africa and
Arabia two thousand years ago, and he
had a huge sense of entitlement, acted like
he was the son of a god and said usehe was
the Son of God, not that anybody here
believed him, or cared, really, but

I took an interest in
this lost soul, wandering around our
country, so far from home, after he had
already spent some time in India, and
you know what that's like, the energy of
that place is so spiritual and ungrounded
and there are holy men everywhere you
look ready to teach you all kinds of
exercises, techniques, tricks, to make you
healthy and holy but our place had a different
sort of energy, much more grounded, and
different traditions for healing and feeling
holy that mixed spirituality with our
belief systems and what we had learned
about the human body and what worked
when people needed healing for one
reason or another. And this dark man
who called himself Jesse or Jesu
or something like that was an
excellent student who absorbed
a lot of information and asked
a lot of good questions and
demonstrated he had the healing
touch as well as the gift of the gab
like a snake charmer he could
sell sand to the desert dwellers
as we used to say and he developed
the ability to do hands-on healing
work like that guy in Japan who
said he invented or created Reiki
and here on Daheishan we like to
stick to our own roots and not
follow the guy who inspired
Christianity or Reiki even though
there's only 1.4 billion of us,
in China, and there are 4 billion
of them around the world and
I don't know how many
Reiki masters there are
but I hear it's getting easier
and easier to do Reiki and other

hands-on healing techniques
because there's something
going on these days and the
world needs a lot of healing ....

That's fascinating, I said. I've heard
there are places in India where,
they say, Jesus visited after he was
born again, and the Japanese say
he moved to their island nation
after that, married a Japanese woman,
and became a farmer, with her help,
then lived a long time without
preaching or healing or telling anyone
who he was or what to do, just growing
vegetables and raising a family, and
his Japanese-Jewish ancestors had
relatively normal lives, avoiding the
attention that would come from
telling anyone who their father or
grandfather or great-great-great
grandfather used to be.

Me: Your perspective on
Christianity is so peculiar,
I said, and not likely to
win you a lot of fans in
the West, and it makes me wonder,
what is your perspective on
the West? You saw the end
of the English Empire, the
rise and fall of the American
Empire, and the start of the
New China, while the Imperialist
Japanese, Germans, or Nazis,
and Russians, came and went
again. What do you make of
all that?

The 100 Year Old Man said,
You like to ask big questions,
don't you, like I'm a big
expert on international
politics and war. I'm just an
old guy who lived most of his life
right here on this mountain.
Sure, I get out, sometimes,
read the newspapers, see the odd
movie, watch a little TV, sometimes
catch some news on the radio,
and now there's the internet,
and I have a good laptop but
the internet connection is slow,
around here, but a lot better than
dial-up, remember that?

I told him that my brother in Canada
still has dial-up and it's slower than
anything in China. He lives in the
country, outside of Penetang, which
is a French part of Ontario near
Midland, a hundred miles north of
Toronto, and he just got satellite TV
last year, after I gave him my old car,

when I moved to China.

That's interesting, he said, because
a lot of Westerners complain about
the speed of the internet in China,
so I thought your part of the world
had the best high-speed internet
connection in the whole world. So
I told him it depends where you live,
in Canada, as southern Ontario has
the ultimate in internet connectivity
but central Ontario, a hundred miles
north of the city, is a different story,
and Northern Ontario is something
else again, although the cities,
North Bay and Sudbury, get better
service, but nothing in the world beats
Toronto, down south ....

That's the biggest city in Canada? he said.
Toronto? The provincial capital? And the
nation's capital is in the same province,
called Ontario? But Ottawa is not such a
big city? And Toronto has 2.5 million
people, but Dalian has six million, and
it's not one of our big cities.

Yeah, yeah, I know, I said. The province
we are in, here in China, has the same
population as all of Canada, and all our
cities put together wouldn't have the
same population of one of China's
biggest cities, like Shanghai, Beijing,
Hong Kong ....

And who are the leaders of your
country and your biggest city?
he asked me. Who was elected by
your multi-party democratic
federal election system and your
no-party but democratic

municipal system?

I hesitated, before I answered, so
he answered for me, as it was a
rhetorical question, anyway, and
he wanted to make a point about
the relative merits of a one party
and multi-party system that gave
China a strong, stable, central
government, year after year,
decade after decade, which we in
the West thought had too much
power, while we had a Prime
Minister, Stephen Harper, and the
mayor of our biggest city, Rob Ford,
who were elected democratically but
appeared to be incredibly unpopular
with the people, frequently ripped apart
by the free press, but elected again and
again anyway. And didn't it appear as
though the prime minister wanted to
take away democratic rights and
freedoms and centralize power in
Ottawa and make a lot of money
turning Canada into an energy
power, even a super-power, selling
oil and other resources, mostly
tar sands bitumen, to the U.S.A.
and China, if they could build
pipelines and ports to transport it
to the two nations with the biggest
economies in the world? And wasn't
China moving fast to overtake the
U.S.A. in terms of GDP and the other
measures of the wealth of nations?

That was when he invited me up to
his place, on another mountain, further
north and east, up by the borders with
North Korea and the old USSR or CCCP,
near Donkeykong, the Chinese city

closest to North Korea, but up in the
mountains, where Taoists like to build
their temples. It will help you put things
in perspective, he promised, so off I went
taking the coastal road from Dalian
almost all the way to North Korea, along
the Yellow Sea, past fishing ports with
and seafood farms, miles and miles of
sea cucumbers, with the Black Mountains
to the north, and it took hours by bus or
car each time but it was worth it to see
some more of the country and a bit of
North Korea and to talk with the
One Hundred Year Old Man.

The prospect of moving to China for a
year or ten freaked me out, at first,
I have to admit, because almost all the news
we get, in the West, about China, is bad
propaganda, not the good news China
likes to promote through its mass media
outlets, but my mind had been changed
from the moment my big Japanese Air Lines
jet cruised by downtown Dalian and I saw
all the skyscrapers, for miles and miles, the
modern home of six million people, and
discovered it was the unofficial capital of
the New China, known as the Paris of
China, or the Hong Kong of the North, but
leaving Dalian for a place on the border with
North Korea and the old CCCP did not
interest me in the slightest.

It's safe, the 100 Year Old Man assured me.
Nobody is going to grab you and drag you into
North Korea and the totalitarian days of
Siberia and the USSR or CCCP are long gone.
North Korea, from my mountain, is a dark place,
at night, as there is no electricity, no city lights,
and there's a lot of undeveloped country, just
wilderness, which is what you like in Canada,
if I'm not mistaken, so you might like
that part of it.

Have you been to North Korea? I asked the
old man. Have you visited that country
recently? Have you seen how it has changed
over the past century? Do you really want to
live next door and do I really want to go there
for a visit? I told him that it made me nervous,
going up there, to the corner of China that
bordered on North Korea and the old
Soviet Union as we in the West heard
nothing but horror stories about what
life was like there, with prison camps
inside countries that were like prison

camps but the old Taoist just grinned
and assured me that the USSR was
no longer the USSR and the borders
were well-guarded, nobody was crossing
into China from Russia or Korea or
going the other way without a great deal
of trouble and paperwork and official
forms as well as visas and passports
so I had nothing to worry about, it would
be just like travelling to any other part of
China, for me, like going to Beijing or
Shanghai for the weekend, or even
Hong Kong, only there were no huge
cities in the north-east, it was more
rural with fishing villages and small
towns in the mountains and a lot of
farms, all the way from Dalian to the
borders. I had travelled up north, from
Dalian to Anshen and Liaoyang, two
cities close to the provincial capital,
Shenyang, and I was looking into
weekend or week-long trips to Seoul,
the capital of South Korea, and Tokyo,
Japan, as they were only around an
hour away from Dalian, by plane, but
I knew lots of people I worked with had
taken the trip up the coast to the border
with North Korea and one guy I knew
went bird-watching up there, leading
trips for bird-watchers who wanted to
add to their life lists by exploring an
area not that many people visited, so
I tried to get over my fears and my
prejudices and forget about the history
of the Cold War, which I grew up with,
and I got organized for a trip up the
coast through a landscape that looked like
the setting for the movie and TV show
called MASH, which stood for
Mobile Army Support Hospital, which
was a concept created by a Canadian

surgeon during the Spanish Civil War,
which he took to China in the 1930s
and which was made famous by the
American movie and TV show, starting
with a big movie starring the Canadian
actor Donald Sutherland, who was
currently famous for his role in
The Hunger Games and whose son
was the star of 24, the American TV
series about a counter-terrorism unit
in the U.S.A. of the future when
America was under attack from
all sides, apparently, and from within,
and my little trip along the coast
of China between the Black Mountains
and the Yellow Sea from Dalian to
Donkeykong was a walk in the park
compared to MASH or 24 or
The Hunger Games as the present
in Dongbei or north-east China was
very peaceful, unlike the past in
this region or the present or future
of the U.S.A. And of course I have to say
Canada should be the model for all
these places at all times as it is a
peaceful country and I could not help
noticing the landscape of China, in the
north-east, reminded me of Canada,
especially the Lake Country north of
Toronto, where I come from, on the other
side of the planet.

From the Chinese side of the river separating
the two countries, what you can see of North
Korea is misleading. The bridge that used to
connect China and Korea was blown up by the
American airforce during World War Two and
there was little left of it and what was left on the
Korean side was hidden by a big ferris wheel
so that if you took a picture of the place you
captured a scene that turned your photograph

into North Korean propaganda.

It's hard for a Westerner to get into North Korea, much easier for someone like me, from China, to get a visa and go for a visit, but all tourists are taken to the same places, which you've probably read about in a graphic novel or seen on TV or in a movie .... There's a hotel on an island and a highway that takes you to places the government wants you to see, and you have an escort who is part tourist guide and part soldier, not to mention a member of the communist party that runs the government, so you don't really get to see much of the country in a way that would let you know what everyday life is like for the North Koreans, but we all know a lot about that, anyway, thanks to the reports of a few people who have been able to get out.

If you are a Westerner in China and you want to
go to North Korea, you have to apply for a visa and
then go up north to Harbin, in the next province,
and wait for word while getting ready to go, go,
go, and after you pay for your trip you will be
escorted to the border and across and everywhere
you go in North Korea and it's difficult to arrange
but not impossible and you will see a little bit of
the country, you will not be free to wander all
over, as you are in China or Canada or most of
the rest of the world. Harbin, a city up north, has
a big reputation, now, and a long history, as
it used to be a small, isolated place, with a
connection to Siberia, and now it is a big city
with some Russian influence and a famous
winter carnival rivalling the big one in
Quebec City, with lots of ice sculptures and
skating and hockey, and it is also the place
to go if you want to take a trip to North Korea
as connections have been made there and
in China it is all about making connections
with people and developing relationships as
that is the way, traditionally, that things get done.

As I rode the bus from Dalian to Donkeykong,
I thought a lot about the One Hundred Year Old
Man I was interviewing and how much he
reminded me of a father figure I had at home,
if not my own father, as I had spent several years
working with a Zen Buddhist monk in eastern
Ontario, a Buddhist monk and Zen master,
originally from Vietnam, now building a
Zen retreat halfway between Toronto and
Ottawa, in the country north of Belleville, on
the edge of the Canadian Shield, so it looked like
Muskoka but was located further south and
the Zen retreat looked a little like
Santa's Village in Bracebridge but with
Asian influenced architecture and Santa Claus
replaced by The Laughing Buddha. My
Zen master taught me how to meditate,

Zen style, 24/7, which helped me relax as
I travelled toward North Korea, thinking about
my father and his life, which was ruined by
World War Two. My father, born the same
year as the One Hundred Year Old Man,
dropped out of university, at the U of T,
to sign up and go overseas as Canada joined
the Allies long before the Americans got
into the war and he spent a long time
in England working on the top secret
radar project which many say won the war
and then he crossed the English Channel
with the Canadians fighting at Juneau
Beach on D-Day and then joined in with
the Canadians who liberated Holland, or
The Netherlands, including the concentration
camp where Anne Frank was held, and
my father came away from World War Two
and some contact with The Holocaust with
a case of TB and undiagnosed PTSD and
he died in his sixties, when I was in my
twenties, and he was an alcoholic after
the war, so I never got to know the veteran
of World War Two that well, and I replaced
him as a father figure with a series of
hockey coaches and high school teachers
and university profs and then a Zen
master and interviewing the One Hundred
Year Old Man made me think about all those
men again, on the trip from Dalian to
North Korea.

I grew up during the Cold War, when the
world lived in the shadow of an undeclared
war between the two superpowers left
standing after World War Two, as the
U.S.A. and the U.S.S.R. competed like
crazy but did not want to go head-to-head
and start World War Three but they
stockpiled enough atomic bombs with
missiles to blow up the whole Earth
many times over and kept the planet
on edge as they argued about which system
was best, democracy or communism,
and after decades of posturing, propaganda,
and proxy wars fought in other countries
with Soviet or American backing, like
North and South Korea and North and South
Vietnam, it was capitalism that brought down
communism and the old USSR and, some
would say, it was capitalism that destroyed
democracy in the USA. And Canada, the big
country located, geographically, between
the U.S.A. and the U.S.S.R., from the American
border up to the North Pole and the Arctic
Ocean, which was the border with Siberia and
the rest of Russia, and the Canadian people were
a lot closer to America but tended to lean
more to the left than most Americans but
backed the USA while secretly hoping something
good would come out of the communist
countries and developing a mixed economy
most Americans thought was far to
socialist for them. And I grew up in a
small town north of Toronto which was the
birthplace of Dr. Norman Bethune, who
helped Canada establish a strong connection
with China and during the Cold War it was
the home of The Northern Book House which
was the largest clearing house for communist
propaganda in North America, where they
created some commie propaganda and
repackaged a lot of propaganda from the USSR.

So I was a guy with a lot of history and
a certain set of prejudices after the Cold War
and I thought about all that as I traveled
from Dalian, in the New China, up to
the border with North Korea.

Have you met anybody who escaped from
North Korea? I asked the One Hundred Year
Old Man. And he said, Sure, but not many.
Once in a while you hear about somebody
getting out and finding there way here, but mostly
they head for the city and they are in a hurry to
get as far away as possible, as fast as they can,
afraid somebody will be after them, of course.
The last time we had somebody here, we tried to
help but there were communication problems,
not just language issues, but other things, as
the guy who escaped appeared to be in shock
because nothing we told him about the way
the world worked made much sense to him and
in the end he stole somebody's motorcycle and
took off, heading toward Dalian and Beijing and
the rest of the world.

After he told me that story, I headed back to
Dalian, and then back to the West, with a
different perspective on everything in the
world, from happiness to religion and
politics as well as history and I guess that's
why you want to talk to a holy man on a
mountain but after your mind is blown and
you feel as though you are a different person
living on a different planet, well, then what
do you do?

When I returned to Canada, after a year in
China, which climaxed with my trip up north to
see the old Taoist guy, I flew from Dalian to
Tokyo to Vancouver and across Canada to
Toronto, on Canada Day, and we flew low, so
I could see the Coastal Mountains, the
Rockies, the Prairies, enormous Lake Superior,
all the city lights of Toronto, and I was warned
about reverse culture shock, how you might feel
out of place in your home and native land after
spending a good deal of time in a different
country with a completely different history and
culture and worldview. But that's what travel
is for: It's up to you to try to put your newly
expanded worldview into some sort of
perspective so the world makes sense to you.

I rented a car for a month, for a thousand bucks,
and drove back and forth from Toronto to
cottage country, a hundred miles up north,
up and down Highway 400, with trips to
Muskoka and Midland, Balm Beach on
Georgian Bay, the Muskoka Lakes, and
over to Stratford to see the Shakespeare
Festival and back down to downtown Toronto.
Everything was still completely familiar to
me, of course; I could still find my way
through the city and all over southern
Ontario and Central Ontario and Western
Ontario, but I didn't go to the Far East
of Ontario, where I used to go, to re-visit
the Zen Forest, and I had no need for
maps or GPS or MapQuest or Google Maps
and I had a good time talking to family and
old friends but every now and then my mind
wandered back to China, especially to my
conversations with the 100 Year Old Man on
Daheishan or Grand Monk Mountain and
up by the border between China, Korea, and
Russia, especially when I read the local
newspapers, which seemed completely

self-involved and unworldly, and when I
caught a couple of Hollywood movies,
Tammy and Sex Tapes, about contemporary
life in America, the U.S.A., the big country
a bit below us, which made it look hopelessly
materialistic and filled with the kind of
people Buddhists call "hungry ghosts",
which are creatures with big mouths,
narrow throats, distended bellies, who
can't get enough, always want more, and
are terribly unhappy. And how can they be
so unhappy, living in the heartland of the
American Empire, the richest place on
Earth, on the other side of the world from
the 100 Year Old Man's mountain over-
looking North Korea and the old USSR?

It's a naive question, of course; there are
lots of reasons to be unhappy in the U.S.A.
during the decline of the American Empire,
and commercial movies made in Hollywood
are not intended to be accurate indicators of
anything other than what some movie producers
think will sell well and make them a lot of
money. Even so, those movies and my
travels up and down Highway 400 made me
think long and hard about everything I
experience on the other side of the world,
especially the words of the 100 Year Old Man.

While I was back in Canada, I read the
newspapers, the way I used to, picking up
the Toronto Star and The Globe And Mail,
looking at the Toronto Sun and the National
Post, checking out NOW Magazine, and
also the Canadian version of TIME magazine,
and I caught some TV news, mostly CITY,
CBC, CTV, and Global, with some CKVR TV, up
north, and I listened to the car radio, mostly
CBC, again, but also The Moose, from Muskoka,
and I continued to get most of my news from
online sources, and I noticed that the U.S.A.
still dominated the news in Canada and
so-called news about American celebrities
got more attention than politicians and
American politicians got a lot more air time
than Canadians, so I heard all about President
Obama and not much about Prime Minister
Harper and a lot about Hilary Clinton, who
looked like the next president of the U.S.A.,
the first female president of the U.S., following
the first black or Africa-American president,
and she was getting a lot more attention than
Justin Trudeau, the son of the Honourable
Pierre Elliot Trudeau, the son of a former
Canadian Prime Minister who looked as though
he would be the next Canadian Prime Minister,
and Toronto Mayor Rob Ford was still making
headlines, as he had all year, and for the past
couple of years, but it was no longer for
smoking crack or getting drunk, it was for
a picnic he was hosting in Scarborough,
called Ford Fest, to kick off his campaign
to ge re-elected, but the polls said both
John Tory and Olivia Chow were way ahead
of him and more likely to get elected.
After a year in China, election races and
party politics and short-lived governments
with majorities or minorities no longer
held my fascination, the way they did for
many decades before.

China changes you, they say, and you don't
change China, because it's just so big and
there are so many people and it has over
five thousand years of history and it's a
giant on a gigantic continent, but I never
felt that way while I was there. I felt as though
I was in the unofficial capital of the New
China and it was changing quickly as the
history of the last century was taking
the Middle Kingdom from the communist
revolution through a late industrial
revolution to a consumer revolution and
the West was missing that story as the
many news stations were not reporting on
the recent changes as they were hung up
on China's past and worried about a big
communist country taking over the world
even though the China I saw did not appear
to have any aspirations of taking over
anything, except maybe a couple of small
islands they claimed along with Japan,
and some air space to go along with it,
and China appeared to be more interested
in exploring space than taking over the
planet Earth, so I don't know what the
West was worried about. I got the
impression China wanted to be China
and not become more like the West and
China wanted the West to remain like
the West, so millions of Chinese people
who could now afford to travel the world
would be able to visit a place that was
quite different than the place where they
lived, and not many people were talking about
changing the world by combining the best
of the Far East and the West, although
there was some movement in the world of
medicine, integrating new Western medical
techniques with ancient Chinese medicine
and what about the traditional medicine

of India, I wondered, but who was
talking about that?

I enjoyed my time in Toronto, Muskoka,
Midland, Georgian Bay, and Stratford, but
I have to say I missed China, or
the New China, or Dalian and Jinshitan,
where I live, as Dalian is the Paris of China,
and I missed Daheishan, in Kaifaqu, or the
Development Zone beside the
Free Trade Zone in the new city that
used to be called Port Arthur and was
once part of Manchuria and has seen
so much history over the past
five thousand years.

Canada looks like a new, young, empty
country, in comparison. My trip from
Vancouver to Toronto showed me a
vast land with lots of mountains and
wilderness and prairies with enormous
farms and a lake with an incredible
amount of fresh water and my trips
inside China showed me a huge country
with a lot of land dedicated to
greenhouses and fish farms as they have
a lot of people to feed. And when I
contemplate Canadian history and
the history of China, North America
and Asia, it is like comparing two
worlds, separate planets, it's almost
impossible to comprehend they are
just on opposite sides of the same
planet and we share one world and
we are all just people on the planet
Earth. How I look forward to
going back, returning to China,
resuming my life there, but I wonder
why. Is it just because I am rich there
and not rich here? Is it because of the
times we live in, my timing, finding a
job that pays in Canadian dollars when
the Canadian dollar goes quite far in
China? How will it look when Chinese

currency rises?

The CIA describes the government of China as
authoritarian, not even high authoritarian, never
mind totalitarian, but, frankly, after a year
here, I have to say I've seen no signs of it, except
in the eyes of certain paranoid Canadians who
see signs of conspiracy everywhere. Who lives on
the fifth floor of our apartment buildings? they say.
There's nobody living there because those
apartments are used by the censors who monitor
our e-mails and our use of the internet. And
on certain anniversaries they say the
internet is slowed down or even stopped
so the government can prevent people from
organizing big protests online using
social media. But this isn't 1984! It's a brave
new world, with fantastic people in it, all
over China, and I love it here, and I'm a
freedom-loving, liberal, guy who is comfortable
with chaos and anarchy, which, frankly, I've
seen much more evidence of here in China
in 2013 and 2014, like reading a novel by
the Nobel Prize winning novelist Mo Yan.

I know the 100 Year Old Man's secrets
and how to live a long and happy life
with good health or what the Chinese call
"jin-chi-sheng", after a year in China,
but after one month back in North America
it appears to me that it is all about
one thing, and that one thing is
making money.

When I ask my best friend in Canada
what she wants, if I can get her anything,
she always says the same thing:
"A million dollars". And I think
everybody in Toronto and the rest of
Ontario and Canada would say
the same thing. Or, since a million isn't
what it used to be, they might say
"a billion dollars". But what would the
100 Year Old Man say? That's what
I learned in China this year.

Did the One Hundred Year Old Man
have a name, an English name as well as
a Chinese name? Did he really exist?
Or was he a figment of my imagination?
Was he a hallucination? Did I imagine
the whole thing? Was I talking to myself?
Was I having a conversation with a dragon?
Did the 100 year-old Taoist guy ask me to
keep him anonymous, as well as his location
in Dongbei, or north-east China, so he was
not overwhelmed with visitors and requests
for information about healing, health, and
happiness, not to mention the Taoist
bedroom arts? Is this Eat, Pray, Love,
a travel book with information about
real people so millions of Americans can
hit the road and travel to China so they, too,
can have a life-changing experience that
leads them to a long and happy life full of
love?

Was the One Hundred Year Old Man
married? Did he outlive one wife and
take another? Was he celibate, like a
monk? Did he write any books? Does he
have a website? Is he on Facebook?
Are you crazy? Do you need a
guidebook to lead you to love,
healthy, happiness, and longevity?

Note: I wrote this little book, just
50 pages, a long poem with some
depth, over four days in July in
Canada, after nine months in
China, while in Toronto and Midland,
or Penetanguishine, or the country
outside of Penetang, and I finished it
on Sunday at Georgian Downs, in the
gazebo beside the race track and
Highway 400, listening to Elvis Presley on
a great set of loundspeakers with a feed from
Graceland called Elvis Radio playing nothing
but Elvis songs, the big hits and a few I'd never
heard before, which gave me more perspective
on my experience in China and my meetings
with the One Hundred Year Old Man who was
a Toaist priest who told me all about being
happy, healthy, and living a long time, as
well as the Taoist Bedroom Arts. Elvis is
singing "take my heart, take my whole life too,
for I can't help falling in love with you ..." on
the station that says "We don't just remember
Elvis, we never forgot!" Of course you know what
I'm thinking: What would the old Taoist guy
make of Elvis, Graceland, the U.S.A. today,
President Obama, Prime Minister Harper,
Mayor Rob Ford, Highway 400, Georgian Bay,
Balm Beach, "Your Cheating Heart" and
"If I'm A Fool For Loving You"?

While I was in Canada, I went up north to
my brother's place on Georgian Bay and
stayed for a few days of swimming and
corn on the cob and Ontario field tomatoes
and the weather turned on us so I only
got in the water once but I went for a
long walk the next day and it gave me
the perfect ending for this book. At my
brother's place on Penetanguishine Bay
he has a stretch of the beach, owned
communally with a dozen other home
owners and cottagers and they have a
long dock from Dock In A Box from the
shore to a spot about one hundred yards
out, where the water is up to your
waist, and while I was walking along
the beach on Saturday, instead of
swimming, as it was good hiking weather
but terrible for swimming, like
September, not July, in this part of
the country, what did I spy at the end
of the dock? It was difficult to make out
from shore but it looked oddly like a
walker, the device with four wheels and
two handles with a seat and basket
you use when you are almost ready for a
wheelchair. It reminded me of the time,
just a year and a half ago, when I got a
walker, after a doctor told me I would
never walk again, or work again, and
that I was going to die. I laughed at him
and walked out then worked my way
back to work, step by step, stage by
stage, and I will never forget what a great
joy it was when I got a walker, so I could
be more mobile and go grocery shopping
and use it to start getting back in shape,
and there was an even greater moment of
joy when I got rid of the walker, returned it
to the place where I got it, as I graduated
to canes, and then started walking on my own

again. And I was thinking, again, how funny
it was that a neurology emergency specialist
in Northern Alberta, Canada, told me I was
going to die but a year later my doctor in
China told me I was strong and healthy as a
man half my age and I would live a long time
and then I hiked up Daheishen, climbing
1,300 stairs to the top of Big Monk Mountain.
But then I realized I had better investigate
the black walker abandoned at the end of
my brother's dock on Penetanguishine Bay
of Georgian Bay. Why would anyone leave a
walker out there?

As I walked out toward the end of the dock,
I noticed the gate by the shore was left
unlocked, which was very unusual, and the
black thing on the dock turned out to be
what I thought it was, what I guessed, what
I didn't want it to be: somebody's black
walker, folded up and abandoned, lying on
its side, on the dock, with nobody around to
claim it. And you have to ask yourself: Who
takes a walker to the beach? Who leaves a
walker on a dock and swims away? Could
somebody have gone on a boat trip, got
picked up, and left their walker on the dock?
Or was it what it looked like? Suicide.

I stood at the end of the dock and looked down
into the water. I looked all over the lake. I looked
down through the slats in the dock to see if
somebody was floating under the dock. Usually,
dead bodies float. Unless you put rocks in your
pockets. I thought of Virginnia Woolf. I thought
about other writers who have killed themselves:
Sylvia Plath and Ernest Hemingway are never
far from my mind. I kicked off my Crocs,
dropped my blue jeans, pulled off my tee-shirt,
and climbed into the water to look around and
under the dock. The ladder leading from the

dock into the water had been let down and left
down, suggesting someone had gone swimming,
or had used the ladder, after using their walker,
to get into the water so they could drown.

Suicide by drowning is fairly easy and fast but
they say freezing to death is better as you just
fall asleep in the cold and never wake up as you
are frozen so you stop breathing and your blood
stops pumping and all your bodily functions
slow down and then stop while you are dreaming.
Drowning, they say, is more difficult, as you
go down for the third time and your life passes
before your eyes, and panic sets in with a big
rush of adrenaline. But there were no signs of
a body or a struggle or anything unusual
under the water, including the area under
the dock. I swam around with my eyes open,
underwater, looking for a deadman with his
pockets full of stones. I was relieved that I
did not find anything but worried because
I did not find anything and was left with this
mystery: Why was there a walker left at the
end of the dock used by swimmers?

I phoned 911 and waited around while an
emergency response team drove out from
the town to my brother's place in the country,
about a half an hour, and then talked to one of
them while the others did what I did: walked
out to the end of the dock, looked at the walker,
looked in the water and under the dock, got in
the water and did a sweep of the area, and
came back with the same results I got: It was
a mystery. Who left a walker at the end of the
dock? Did somebody end their life out there?
It made me think of the One Hundred Year Old
guy I met inChina, on the other side of the world,
who lived on top of a mountain in an area that
looked something like my brother's place on
Georgian Bay. -- Opposites at opposite ends of

the earth.

I hate to leave you hanging but I never did find out
what the story was behind that walker left at the
end of the dock.

Soon I will be flying back to China.
I have my elecltronic ticket and my
passport and visa all ready to go
and I know my departure and arrival
times for Toronto, Beijing, and
Dalian. It took me one long day,
about 28 hours, to fly from Dalian
to Toronto, but it will take me
three days to go back again. There's
a layover in Beijing, the big city with
the world's biggest airport, but that
doesn't bother me, now, unlike
a year ago, when I was flying
across the Pacific Ocean for the
first time. It will be easier the
second time and the third time and
all the other times as I fly back and
forth from Dalian to Toronto by
way of Vancouver and Tokyo or
Beijing or maybe Seoul, Korea,
I know the big airports are laid out
so well a champanzee could find
the way and there's enough
signage in English and people
who speak a few words of English
to get you through as the American
Empire that followed the British
Empire still has a huge influence
internationally, including Asia,
and China is learning English fast,
thanks to a lot of teachers like me.
As soon as I get back to my
part of China, which is Dalian,
the unofficial capital of the
New China, also known as
the Paris of China or
the Hong Kong of Northern
China or the Jewel of Dongbei
or north-eastern China, and
Jinshitan, or Golden Pebble Beach,
where I live and work, one of the

first things I do, after visiting my
favourite doctor, for acupuncture
with fire cupping and moxibustion
plus tunai or finger needling, will be
to hike up Daheishen, 1,300 steps,
on the spiritual path linking several
Taoist temples, some with big
Buddhist influences, and then
I'll take a motorcycle taxi over to
the ancient Taoist temple, so old
it pre-dates Taoism, and I will look for
my double, my doppelganger, my
Chinese twin, the One Hundred
Year Old Man.

My doctor will ask me about my
trip to Canada, my summer
vacation in the country north
of Toronto. Did you abuse your
back? she will say. Did you swim
in cold water? Play golf? Eat a lot of
rich North American food? Did you
shovel snow? Catch cold? Or did you
stick to your Chinese diet and sleep
on a hard bed and take the Chinese
herbs I gave you and wear the
herbal patches so you get healthy
or healthier so you have good
jing-chi-shen? I will assure her that
I did not play golf or gain a lot of
weight and the water wasn't too
freezing cold. And then I will
hike up Daheishan again, go over to
the ancient Taoist complex, sit
cross-legged in front of the dragon
with the spring water pouring
out of his mouth and into the
koi pond with one million fish and
I will meditate on the meaning of it all:
Canada and China, the USA and the
USSR, the East and West, the One

Hundred Year Old Man and the
Two Thousand Year Old Man, Muskoka
and North Korea, the decline of the
American Empire, after the British
Empire, and the rise of China. I saw
TIME magazine online with a cover story
about the NEW Cold War as America
worries about Putin's Russia taking over
Ukraine and that makes me wonder about
the border between the New China and
the old USSR and the advice my Zen
master and the old Taoist guy gave me,
not to mention Margot Anand and
Mantak Chia, about how important it is
to meditate and make love, not war, as
we used to say. Meditate and make love,
not war. Let's all remember that
is the way to peace, love, happiness,
health, and longevity.

P.S. Canada, from China, had a very peculiar
profile as the USA was always in the news but
we never heard much about Canada unless
we looked for it or it was bad news about
Toronto Mayor Rob Ford or Canadian
pop star Justin Beiber, who performed in
Dalian just before I got there and got in
a lot of trouble in Europe and the U.S.A.
after that so that many Americans were
calling for his deportation, "Send him back
to Canada", and hockey fans in Canada and
the USA wanted to make bets about the
Toronto Maple Leafs or Montreal Canadiens
in the Stanley Cup play-offs facing teams in
the USA with the loser taking Beiber, but
then there was an all-American NHL
Stanley Cup Final with NYC versus LA,
the Rangers versus the Kings, and we knew
the team with the most Canadians would
win, but it was a little hard to follow in
China, half a world away, because of the
time zone differences, like day and night,
like a lot of the differences between
Asia and the West. From China, Canada looks
like a hockey-obsessed country led by a
Prime Minister hell-bent on selling tar sands
oil quickly but frustrated in his efforts to
build oil pipelines to take the thick crude
or bitumen to the U.S.A. or through B.C.
to ports with oil tankers from China.

From Dalian, on a clear day, from a high spot,
such as Daheishan, you can see a long line of
supertankers, three abreast, on the horizon in
the Yellow Sea, taking an incredible amount of
material goods made in China to markets around
the world, heading for Vancouver and Seattle and
L.A. and Australia and everywhere and somewhere
there's another line of supertankers taking raw
materials from around the world to China
with a lot of coal and iron ore from Australia

and wood from Canada and they are waiting
on the arrival of Canadian oil.

Will China take over the world? everyone is
asking, in the West, but not in China, where
everyone is asking, How do I get a visa to go
visit the West. China does not appear to have
any aspirations to take over the world, so
far as I can see, but the country called the
Middle Kingdom would be willing to take on
the role of leadership, if required by
the rest of the world, to show everyone
how to fix their economy and feed billions
while lifting many millions out of poverty.

Personally, I believe Chinese women will
take over China and then China will take
over the world. But that's another story
for another day and not something
I discussed with the One Hundred Year Old
Taoist guy on the mountain.

About the author ....

Canadian author Martin Avery, Hons. B.A., B.Ed., M.F.A., A.Q., Hons. Spec. Eng., D.I.S.H., now living in China, wrote 100 books set in the West and is now working on 100 books set in the East. After winning the Balzac Award for poetry, he was inspired to write 100 books, like Balzac, called The Human Comedy.

He was the Arts Department Head of the high school in Norman Bethune's hometown and is now English Department Head at Maple Leaf in Dalian, China. He's the founder of A Novel Marathon, the Muskoka Novel Marathon, The Great Canadian Winter Novel Marathon, the Toronto Novel Marathon, et cetera.

In addition to being an author and educator, he is a Reiki master, Zen meditation teacher, and qigong instructor.

He won the Most Prolific Poet Award at the Scugog Poetry Marathon and the Balzac Poetry Award.

The Great Wall Of China Books Series

1. From Bethune's Birthplace To The People's Republic Of China (memoir)
2. Swimming To China (poetry)
3. Mo Yan And Me (short novel)
4. Far Away, Dalian, Far Away (travel)
5. A Trip Around Lake Muskoka With Norman Bethune (short novel)
6. In Love And War
7. Chinese Kisses (poetry)
8. My Chinese Metamorphosis (poetry)
9. Hockey Night In China (non-fiction)
10. An Intro To Acupuncture And TCM (non-fiction)
11. Norman Bethune's Tears Cure Cancer (novel)
12. Bethune Returns To China (novel)
13. Bethune's Time (novel)
14. The Bethune Trilogy: A Trip Around Lake Muskoka With Norman Bethune, Bethune's Tears Cure Cancer, Bethune Returns To China
15. Good News From China (found poetry)
16. Suzanne Takes You Down (novel)
17. The Woman Who Was Picked Up By A Monk (poetry)
18. Bethune Buttons (poetry)
19. Dear China: Love Letter Poems
20. Dalian: A Long Poem (poetry)
21. The Way Of The Dragon (novel)
22. Past And Future Lives In China (fiction)
23. Love And Death In China (duology)
24. The Beijing-Vancouver Express: Connecting Toronto To Dalian, China to Canada
25. Dalian: A Long Poem
26. Toronto: A Long Poem
27. Toronto And Dalian: Two Long Poems
28. The Timeless Universal Etheric Library (poetry)
29. Oh Canada: A Long Poem On Canada Day
30. Holocaust Healing (novel)
31. My Chinese Enchantment (poetry)
32. Gravenhurst And China: A Long Poem
33. Crazy For Stratford: A Very Long Poem
34. A Midsummer Night's Dream In Stratford: A Very Long Poem
35. Stratford, China: A Long Poem
36. The One Hundred Year Old Man I Met In China: A Long Poem

Poetry

1. Poetry Night In Muskoka
2. How To Make Love In A Muskoka Chair
3. Al Purdy's Ghost
4. Twilight At The Museum
5. What Balzac Said
6. Identical Strangers
7. Zen Forest Haiku
8. Celebrating Global Warming
9. Ya Ya Yakupov!
10. Swimming To China
11. Chinese Kisses
12. My Chinese Metamorphosis
13. Good News From China
14. The Woman Who Was Picked Up By A Monk
15. Bethune Buttons
16. Dear China: Love Letter Poems
17. Dalian: A Long Poem
18. Toronto: A Very Long Poem
19. Toronto And Dalian: Two Very Long Poems
20. Oh Canada: A Long Poem On Canada Day
21. Canada From China: A Long Eulogy
22. My Chinese Enchantment
23. Gravenhurst And Bethune And China: A Long Poem
24. Crazy About Stratford: A Very Long Poem
25. A Midsummer Night's Dream In Stratford: A Very Long Poem
26. Stratford, China: A Long Poem
27. The One Hundred Year Old Man I Met In China: A Long Poem